intimate landscape

THE FOUR CORNERS IN POETRY AND PHOTOGRAPHY

intimate landscape

THE FOUR CORNERS IN POETRY AND PHOTOGRAPHY

Photographs by Claude Steelman
Poems by Rosemerry Wahtola Trommer

Photographs by Claude Steelman
Poems by Rosemerry Wahtola Trommer

ISBN 978-1-887805-30-8
Library of Congress Control Number: 2009929659

"Increase Your Thirst" first appeared in *Base Camp Colorado*, Volume 2 Number 7
"Longing" first appeared in *Encore* 2007
"Cartography" first appeared on *A Prairie Home Companion,* April 2008
"Treasure Hunt in the Woods" first appeared in *Monitor Magazine*, Summer 2008
"In Talking About the Present" first appeared in *Four Corners Free Press*, April 2007
"Trying to Be an Optimist on a Cold, Brittle Day" first appeared in *Come Together, Imagine Peace* (Bottom Dog Press), 2008
"While Trying to Fit in a Hike before Arriving on Time to my Meeting" first appeared in *Encore* 2008

www.thedurangoheraldsmallpress.com

Printed in Korea

To my wife Katie,
for all her love and support.
— CS

To Eric, my partner
in falling in love with this world.
— RWT

invisible note left beside the vase

I wanted to bring you
the pale pink perfume
of the wild rose
and so cut it from beneath aspen runes.
It nodded, as if agreeing
to be a doorway, a portal
for silence where the words
are not what matters
as much as the gift of opening.

intimate

WHAT SKIN KNOWS

dare

Oh! To walk right up to the waterfall,
       to feel the cold spray and not hesitate a second.
To rush into chill flash of brrr yes strong harsh slap
       of free fall, long thin wicks of white snow thrill stinging,
the winter still singing its cold, cold clear voice.
       To be here. To be here and not anywhere else.
To let the mind know only what skin knows.
       To applaud the delight in stiff shock. To laugh.

And then when limbs can no longer succumb
       to onslaught of drift turned to wave turned to drop,
to sit on gray rocks and let sun enter in,
       to wring the heart clean and be emptied again.
To rhyme our joy with no slant of wish.
       To open our lips, unsure of whatever might enter us next.

to fall deeper in love with the world

Sit with lichen
        longer than comfort allows.

The urge to move must rise and pass,
        rise and pass, must pass.

Frustration breeds.
        Sit. Sun. Rain. Snow.

Until little by little
        the wanting is gone

and all that remains
        is sitting with lichen.

increase your thirst

Love whispers in my ear ... make yourself My fool. —Rumi

Today it was the sharp stinging voice of nettles
that suggested to me: Be a fool.

For walking off the traveled path
into dappled shade of aspen grove,

wildflowers buried me up to my chest
and I waded bare belly, bare legs, sandaled feet,

through wide umbels of cow parsnip's generous emerald
and wound around corn lily stalks unspiraling.

Every leaf still glistened with last night's rain,
and in seconds, I, too, was wet to dripping,

dripping, inhaling damp sweetness, the sultry bog smell
of long shade and mud-shush and slow seeping pools.

I inhaled as if I'd finally learned how to breathe,
felt the air grab my lungs and shake me, shake me from the inside into joy, joy that limbs might move
                    through deep forests and into hushed glades of bloom.

                    And not even trying to hide amidst midsummer leaves
                        were tall spears of nettle, brutally green, abundant,

                            serrated, pointed, rising like steeples,
                            staking their right to survive.

                    No way to steer through so many stems.
        two choices: turn back toward the path or wade through them.

                    And who but a fool would submit to be stung
                    for the chance to briefly romp with fecundity.

                        Four hours later, the brisk sting of welts
                        finally settles in the thick skin of memory,

                    and I have been shaken into breathing again,
                        greedy lungs, not sipping, but gulping.

when feeling stuck

Go to the shadowed place
           where the waterfall has frozen
                  into sharpened idiom.

The white-spirited frolic
          now captive, blue-fanged.
                Stand here. Feel how weight accumulates.

But the earth revolves
          so slightly and tomorrow
                sunlight edges nearer.

remedy for almost anything

In a field of wild sunflowers there's no gap
where sister regret might slip in.

Feel how her woeful gray weight
sheds like old skin until all that matters

is the way brown-eyed faces nod and nod
as if saying yes and yes and yes.

Come stand in the center
of endless consent.

If you have been weeping,
bring tears.

How soon a new root grows in you
and slowly gold uncurls from what was dust.

Turn toward your shadow, regardless its length,
and see how blooms dapple its lines.

This is one way we learn to accept:
with gentleness nodding on every side.

pleasure lesson: we do the inexplicable

Though our teeth clench and chatter,
skin prickles in goose bumps
and torsos shudder, contract,
we do not leave the frozen pond.

We're lured to the sauna,
the sun, the lover,
something to warm us
and soothe the shiver.

Then our heads, so wise,
shake their dissent.
And our bodies, giddy,
dive in again.

start somewhere

When you listen to the story of the white birds
that skimmed the morning drive,
imagine how they might have taken flight
in your wintry blood, if only
you, too, had remembered to look up.

You must sit with the eight brown leaves
that still cling to the naked shrub
and recognize your own dry dreams,
how they, too, were once green
and gathered the sun into succulence.

When did you let your thoughts
become stiff knuckled,
forget how to surrender to opening?

And where is the smell of spring?
And how might you slip your breath
into the rhythm of snow melting
drip   drip   drip
and become the rich song
the one-note crow wishes to sing?

Regret is the sister of longing.
They both fall in love with their long blue shadows,
mesmerize themselves with their lonely dance.

If you sit long enough by the naked plants,
you will see how the sticks
bare their own bald grace,

how sometimes the most powerful prayers
begin as skeletons.

or perhaps wash it all away

He gave her a beautiful
box full of ash.
Everyday she imagines
the lovely trees
they once were,
tries to plant them again
in the same dry soil.
If she cries enough,
might they take root,
go deeper?

intimate

COME NEAR

couldn't we all use a miracle?

Above tree line the heart can breathe.
At last, a space that does not try to contain it,
a landscape sufficiently vast for love and love and love
and oh, says the heart, at last you get it,
the map is only a rendering,
and the pleasure is in the wandering
and the miracle is in the noticing.

the day is here, is now

Already the rose hips hang softened and red,
the shade of abundance come to an end.

Not a test. All things move toward ripening
and frost comes when it will.

Soon these autumnal rubies
fall from their strings

or shrivel like something forgotten.
And what will we make of the loss,

we who rush only toward happiness,
can we say to the frost, *Come near,*

I've been growing a beautiful garden within
for you to enter and rearrange.

in the meadow

There is no bell
        in the tower
                of thought.

Hours are forgotten.
        Sun sings high
              and the wide field

appeals to deer.
        Snatches of goose music
            alert the air,

and the only thing to do
        is not do.
               There is no work harder.

where you're planted

I too would like to crawl beneath
      a low sandstone lip and lodge
            myself in the loose sand, away from the light
and the restless wind—the nagging wind
      that talks all night, all night and all spring.
            I want to tuck my dreams into a thin seed coat,
reduce them to something tangible and tiny—why
      do they have to be so big? Once
            placed in a desolate corner of desert,
would I dare as the humble red paintbrush
      to put down roots and then blossom
            there, the dream exposed?
Oh spindly petals, the mockery
      of garden peonies or roses, in this barrenness
            any bloom is praiseworthy, any dream a risk.

the familiar pond

Each time trout leap
the pond surface shudders—
concentric circles widening.
Eventually, they dwindle.
The water stills.

A trout leaps again,
his rainbowed body,
elastic, hurls toward sunlight,
mouth agape,
tail ecstatic with flutter.

What in me yearns
for the world beyond

the mind ripples out
seeking edges that contain it.

I wade in cool green depths
of whys and what ifs. Curious.
Wonder deepens over my head.
Fluid and fickle,
light wavers in its bed.

What was clear undulates,
fluctuates like green algae filaments.
And what is that skating the rim
outside reach? Hungry, I leap
and the world begins to shudder.

coyote willow

When the mind grows wild,
        its green-leaved shoots
                pullulate in every margin:
every sidestream, river bank,
        reservoir and ditch
                becomes a fertile foundation

for extending new branches—
        long reddish-brown limbs of ideas,
                tangled but determined,
        hungry for light,
reaching ecstatically
        to form some vague shape—

because any way it can expand,
        it will: persistent, scrappy,
                a rhizomatous marvel
        that even when curbed—
                when scoured by ants, submerged,
beleaguered by drought,

pummeled by hail or whacked to the stub—
                even then it races to the promise of the barren edge
(where you thought you had rendered infertile the soil),
                launches itself like a synaptic bolt
and its green lances slash as if to say *you can't stop me*
        and you can't.

before shouting hallelujah,
reconsider

Oh to be the purple breath
        of pasque flower that rises
                from the snow, the first

to leap, to praise the earth
        with curls of leaf and core of gold
                and startling softness for such chill.

No need to shout or even hum.
        Enough to know the day as swatch of blue,
                as warmth that parts white curtains.

why talk of anything else?

It often starts this way, another day
with the golden yolk of the ambitious list
breaking open in morning's front shirt pocket.

Nothing to do then but take off the shirt,
run stone naked to the pond, tiptoe then launch
and the list is forgotten midst crawdads and blue-eyed grass.

It's electric, this notion that this is it.
And the clunky shoes of what tasks we must do
lose their weight and float toward the sun.

And what if this is it,
this daily waking to weeds unpulled,
and deadlines unmet and furniture yet unstained?

And what if there is nothing more
than rising to sky staring bluely back,
and the certain acceptance of water

which seals vows with ephemeral rings,
and the soiled list which hides in its own yellow cringe,
and the ordinary sun which comes up each morning.

locked in at 80 on I-70

My mind grazes
on the black hum of speed
and eventually gallops

away from four wheels to the north
where the Bookcliff Hills
stitch a barren seam across desert.

On the other side,
wild horses measure days
in sage and wind.

Pictures show explosions
of mane craving upward,
fierce brown chiseled flesh, a battalion of necks.

Sweat-glazed bodies glint against dust.
I listen under the highway hum
for eruptions of unshod hooves,

for keen silver silence of rest.
I imagine hunger,
nights hung with stars.

And while faithful eyes
guide me
through an endless plot

of white dotted lines,
the restless mind runs—
thick muscled and wet,

throat tall, nose keen,
untamable,
refusing to pasture.

intimate

LISTENING IS THE DEEPEST PRAISE

note to self

It's okay to not decide today.
You do not need to run, lungs heaving, legs spent, toward the finish.

There is only one finish.
Walk slow.

See how the snow masks new strawberry leaves,
how yesterday's stream, near-flood, has dwindled to slenderer speak.

You are not behind. There is now.
Today's sky, unable to choose between winter and spring,

elects both, and alternates blue and hail.
The sky does not fuss that it made the wrong choice.

And there will be strawberries, ripened and red.
The stream will rise soon enough in its bed.

Whatever your worry, regardless how gray,
night will still spill uncountable stars.

The river has not made plans for tomorrow.
The strawberries wait for warmth.

In the dictionary, erase the word *late*.
Write in the words, "There are no mistakes."

on deadline, staring out the window

How practical we can be.

We walk the earth so shackled by goals
and manufacture urgency

when there are tall marsh grasses to wander in,
kingfishers braiding the air as they *clack,*

and blackbirds flashing their secret red—
such an abundance of guides so close at hand

to help us get lost more often.

for _____, who died last week

In the face of your death,
joy is a radical act.
Morning mist clings to spruce
while meadows below ring clear.

All through dawn it rained—
first rain of spring—
and each leaf slips
into a new green dress.

The buds on spring willows
still clench like tight fists
and the river trickles lean,
wanting snowmelt's white muscles.

For robins, today suggests
the same red song as yesterday.
The beaver gnaws
at the same lame tree.

The rest of us move through
stations of Wednesday,
waking and working, watching
bluebirds who returned yesterday.

The birds scrounge for twigs—
such tiny nests. We scour
to re-clothe these interminable days
with oddments of joy,

comb each moment
for a scrap of something soft.
With leaf, bud, song, we weave
a morning worth curling into.

one thing after another

This morning it is enough
        that the sunflowers didn't freeze.
                We all need something bright to cling to.

It's so hard to not anticipate frost,
        to let today's gold be gold
                and not imagine it blackened, shriveled on the stalk.

There are days we walk through the field
        when green, green, green is all it knows.
                No hint of chill's shadow, of straw.

There are days the sunflowers nod to us,
        kiss orange every edge of our thoughts.
                Gather those days into armful bouquets.

Now is the only moment we need to trust.
        And when frost comes,
                adjust.

if you were a leaf in the golden fringe

Then the day is a mother
who holds you close,
        and the branch is a father
        who says *let go*,
and the heap below
is the way the world says
        come enter in
        you hail from exceptional parenting.

what I would like to say to you

You do not have to smile.
        Put the brave face in a box.
                Curl your bones into my spiral of hum
and I will make you a home here.

You don't need to tell me about
        what was said and what was not.
                And I will not speak of these things.
I will not speak at all except to say your name.

All around us dead leaves dance
        like brown prayers unloosed from dry lips.
                Mule deer graze at what lies beneath snow;
they tutor us in listening.

Listening is the deepest praise.
        Language is only handfuls of dust.
                For now, let the wind do the singing.
Lay down your head. Shhh.

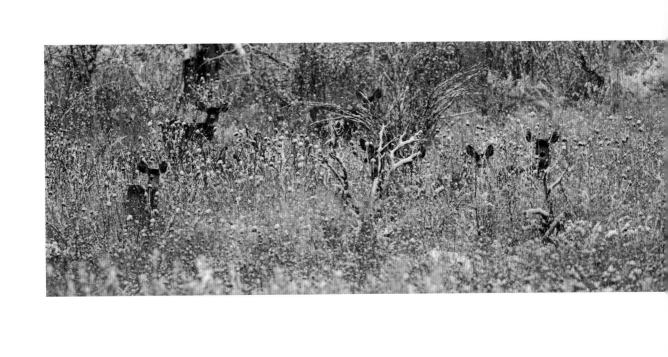

intimate

NO INCH UNSUNG

would it be worth it for that moment?

When we get to the pool at the top of the waterfall
where water rests in slow eddies of clear,
I will ask you to stop and sit with me
on sun-warmed rocks, will linger there
while you tell me everything.
Every thing and every imagining.
And then when the only sound is of water downstream
crashing seventy feet below,
perhaps we will find the place
where all words try to go,
that brilliant verge where everything separates
then returns to a lucid whole.
If we step too close to the edge
we might for a moment become rainbow.

springs eternal

I
would
like
to
find
you
in
some
desert
where
I
would
be
your
only
source
of
water.

treasure hunt in the woods

After three steps into evergreen shade,
  he drops to his knees and begins to furrow.
    It's here, mama, he says. *Let's dig.*

I pick up a knobby spruce twig and poke absently at dirt,
  hoping we can start walking again.
    No, mama, like this. With your hands.

I pretend I don't hear.

He takes my hands in his own, forces them down.
  Fine sand riddles the lace of cold fingers
    and old spruce needles filter, profuse angled wands.

I settle in, sifting and digging up dirt. Making piles.
  No mama, deeper than that, he says,
    scratching with his nails into the hardpan.

I dig deeper, past my desire to keep my hands clean.
  Past whatever I had set out to do. Treasure is cold
    and filled with crooked things that slip through fingers.

makes the heart grow fonder

All day
he was
river song,

and she,
the windows
flung open.

letter to _____

Your laughter carries like ravens
that skim above barren snow
and startle the afternoon into listening.

You laugh louder when you're afraid,
try to cover your fear with a cheerful patina.
You worry when people stare. Let them stare.

I want to find you a field full of snow drift
that echoes your shimmer, let you see how
dense clouds can't extinguish your luster.

You don't need to try to burn more brightly.
I want you to see how I see you, your glorious grays,
how white crests are enhanced by shadowy places.

And when I stare at you long, you will know
it's because I see both your shadow and shine
and how I love to watch you dance that line.

even if the water to cold

Come sit with me
in this small boat
and place your hands
on oars near mine.

How soon the launch disappears.
How soon nothing matters
but wave and sky
and partnering of limbs.

I have stopped fearing
the boat will tip.
We both know
how to swim.

dry time

Tonight
let me
love you
the way
a cactus
flower unfolds:
soft, pink, surprising,
succulent
above
ten thousand spines.

Spines prickle
at air
or anything
that dares
come close.
Blossoms say,
"Look at me.
A little rain
grows
such tenderness."

cartography

I want to know your body as I know
these sandstone cliffs behind our house—take treks
for weeks along your spine, traverse your neck
with slow, exploratory eyes and go
for long excursions in your limbs with no
set plan for how I might get home, except
to know that you will lead me there. I'll step
so lightly, leave no evidence. And oh,
the topo maps I'll make will not be made
of paper but of tune. No rise of you
will be unknown to me, no inch unsung.
I know topographies change by the day,
that wind and water have their way. So true.
A good mapmaker's work is never done.

intimate

LOVING WHAT IS

put me in my place

If nothing delights us, we get mean. —Jan Worth

I come to this alpine meadow for kisses,
how dew does what dew does
with soft morning lips.
I'd walk thirty miles for this,

this damp green communion
beneath aspen dapple
where larkspur spark violet
above white lace umbels.

This is what a body is for,
to be dwarfed by beauty,
to give itself up to a day with no wind
and a bath of dawn light.

And this is why legs learn quickly to clamber,
this is why lungs learn to love the burn.
Because petals unfurl.
Because dew disappears.

while trying to fit in a hike before arriving

on time to my meeting

Today the ducks reminded me to stop.
They did not lead by example,

but because I stopped, I could thrill in details
as they dallied through daily routine:

endless preening of feathers, brown riffle
of wings, crooked arcs of slender green necks.

No there is not time for each purpose on earth,
not seasons enough in one life for everything.

So we turn, turn, turn, turn;
at least the song got that part right.

But seasons always overlap.
The time to mourn and time to dance

are the same time. With the same heart
we keep and cast away. At the same time

we rend and sew, we plant and pluck,
we kill and heal. In each moment,

we breed and we die some small death.
So we turn, turn, turn, turn, and then

stop. Watch ducks. Watch pond rings dissipate.
Stop till we notice how everything turns,

all at once: the pond, the air, the dirt.
When we break down the moment we build it anew,

and in losing ourselves we get.
And in getting it, we see how stopping

is one more small step in the dance
as we turn, turn, turn, turn.

State of the headwaters

Swollen and mud-ruddled
　　　brown murk of residues
　　　　　slosh and befuddle
and dare the banks not to break,
　　　betcha can't hold, betcha can't hold it in,
　　　　　　and it must feel so good to make fun of the walls
and then rush past them all splashscuttlehaste,
　　　wild riot of snowmelt no longer clear
　　　　　　but desperate to get just one inch nearer the ocean,
which this torrent never will reach.
　　　But that doesn't stop it from hurtling toward there.

not worrying who sees
or what they think

Eager to play, spring bumbles in
     like a dizzy bee
          dazed by yellow exuberance
wondering which tree, which stem,
     which blade of new grass to next visit.
          Whirrrrr-whoosh hustles in the first hummingbird,
whip-stridently flirting with petal-some red,
     sweet hussy of fling,
          flippant rush of a thing,
yes! then tides of wings gather
     to jostle for nectar,
          warm air wears their buzz like a hymn.
And what could be better than today to remember
     that we, too, are found in the rush,
          this daily detour toward sweetness and thrill,
this unpredictable swerve of a path on which
     evening enters on gray glimmer of wing so bright
          that even the shadows are listening.

the mudslide reminds me

Surrender.
Dark sky groans downward,
remembers it has roots,
and earth scumbles its clumsy red hands
across the paved highway
as if to mirror a billowing afternoon sky.
I let the rumors of heaven
enter my car's open window,
receive the crazy rain with its ten thousand tongues,
and the doors of my heart turn open,
the flood comes in
and I sing, because that is how it is,
because at least my blood
knows how to be honest,
knows how to praise today,
sludge-muck and schedule-stuck.
But there's somehow always more to surrender
hiding in the bones, the marrow that says
it's work to love this ruthlessness,
to feel the corners disappear,
to watch wide-eyed as afternoon unslopes into evening.

beyond wanting

The leaves don't care what we wear,
don't care what titles we've earned.

They dance with us when we show up.
That makes us worthy enough.

We want so much to be known,
to be lauded for what we've done.

The choir of leaves is chanting, *Come,
abandon your name on the wind.*

keep moving

That's what the elk told me today
as he charged across the snow field.

I had stopped driving the highway to watch,
but my stasis spurred it from grazing to rush.

It reminded me of playing nocturnes by Chopin,
my melody ardent despite awkward hands,

how I love to linger on single notes
which drape like silk sheets between silences.

The urge is to pause on the shoulder of pleasure and cling,
to delay whatever the next measure brings—even if it's more pleasure.

But we don't get to stay, not the nocturne, the elk, the snow, the car,
my longing, your longing, where I've been, where you are.

The field swallows the elk, the eyes rue the trees,
and the wheels find the asphalt and keep moving.

it's time, it's always time

Willows lick banks with wild reds,
      and summer settles like a dog on its lazy haunches
           before curling into fall's frosted nights.

Joy is where we find it, and we find it here,
      re-rooting in one place and loving what is as it veers.
           Breathe deeply, deeply. The air wears tansy perfume.

It is always time to witness. Again and again.
      And if not now, while the west wind licks
           in tongues of renovation, if not now, then when?

in talking about the present

Ooooh, I thought you said *bee here now,*
said the bear who was hungry for honey.
She'd been looking for bees for days, for days,
hoping to follow them home.
All she knew of the present was that
there was not enough sweetness in it
so she sat as quietly as she could,
listening for the distant drone of wings.

after a bad, bad day

I will talk about grief,
but first, I befriend the moon.

See how it has no light of its own,
only empty craters catalogue its measure of space.

Consider how its shadows return.
Reconsider: Shadows lapse.

And tonight the thin cup holds nothing back
as it empties its silver into the pond.

For all this giving,
it shines no less bright.

I will talk about grief, but first
I will see how generous it can be.

trying to be an optimist on a cold, brittle day

So I run faster and race dry leaves,
bend like squirrel grass in wind gusts,
aware that I look like a fool.
Seems to me, and I'm thankful, that skepticism
makes a lousy scarf to warm the neck. Wear wool.

In emptied limbs peals an opera of moon
and the lively brown sparrow rises
to hop along the naked tree, a winged comedy.
We meet the moment, though sparse, though cold.
This is the way we choose to love the world.

Acknowledgments

Once we decided to do a book together,
we knew it wouldn't be easy.

We were right. That didn't stop us from having fun.
We wrote and took pictures anyway.
For many years.

Then we found the folks who could help turn
our playfulness into these pages.
We send huge bouquets of thank yous to:

Lisa Snider Atchison, our designer, for her font
wrestling and out of the rectangle way of thinking.

Elizabeth George Green, our thoughtful editor,
for giving the book its spine and reeling in
any unrulinesses.

Art Goodtimes, for the decades of poetic practice
he brought to the raking of these poems.

Robert Whitson and everyone at
Durango Herald Small Press who (bless them)
chose to publish poems and photography.

AND

The animals and plants, the cirques and the clefts
of this region. May we return to meet them again
and again and again. And again.

Claude Steelman

Claude Steelman's love for the outdoors led him to a career in nature photography. For the past twenty-five years he has traveled from the Arctic to the Central American rainforest capturing the beauty of nature on film. Claude's images have been published in hundreds of publications worldwide, including *National Wildlife* magazine, *Smithsonian* magazine, Sierra Club Calendars, *Field & Stream, Arizona Highways, National Geographic World,* and *Outdoor Life.* Three of his photographs appear on the tails of Frontier Airlines planes. Claude's cinematography has been featured in wildlife documentaries on the Discovery Channel, PBS, and the National Geographic Channel. His other books include *Colorado for the First Time, Durango Country* and *Colorado's Wild Horses,* which is a finalist for the Colorado Book Award.

Rosemerry Wahtola Trommer

Poet and organic fruit grower Rosemerry Wahtola Trommer lives in Southwest Colorado, where she serves as Poet Laureate of San Miguel County. Driven by a passion for connecting outer and interior landscapes, she teaches poetry for Young Audiences, The Aesthetic Education Institute of Colorado and Camp Coca Cola. Her poetry collections include *Holding Three Things at Once,* (a finalist for the Colorado Book Award and finalist for the Colorado Independent Press Association Poetry Award); *If You Listen* (also winner of the Colorado Independent Press Association Poetry Award); *Insatiable,* and *Suitcase of Yeses*, an audio CD. She's anthologized in *What Wilderness This Is* and *Geography of Hope*. Her MA in linguistics is from the University of Wisconsin-Madison. As mother to three children ranging in ages from 0 to 25, she relies on singing for her sanity and performs with a seven-woman a cappella group, Heartbeat.